JORDIN SPARKS

By Michou Kennon

 Gareth Stevens
Publishing

Please visit our website, www.garethstevens.com. For a free color catalog of all our high-quality books, call toll free 1-800-542-2595 or fax 1-877-542-2596.

Kennon, Michou.
Jordin Sparks / by Michou Kennon.
  p. cm. — (Rising stars)
Includes index.
ISBN 978-1-4339-8982-7 (pbk.)
ISBN 978-1-4339-8983-4 (6-pack)
ISBN 978-1-4339-8981-0 (library binding)
1. Sparks, Jordin — Juvenile literature. 2. Singers — United States — Juvenile literature. I. Kennon, Michou. II. Title.
ML3930.S712 K46 2014
921—d23

First Edition

Published in 2014 by Gareth Stevens Publishing
111 East 14th Street, Suite 349
New York, NY 10003

Designer: Nick Domiano
Editor: Therese Shea

Photo credits: Cover, p. 1 Johnny Nunez/WireImage/Getty Images; p. 5 Christopher Polk/Getty Images Entertainment/Getty Images; p. 7 Michael Buckner/Getty Images Entertainment/Getty Images; p. 9 Barry Brecheisen/Getty Images Entertainment/Getty Images; p. 11 Joe Corrigan/Getty Images Entertainment/Getty Images; p. 13 Beyan Nedder/Getty Images Entertainment/Getty Images; p. 15 Evan Agostini/Getty Images Entertainment/Getty Images; p. 17 Kris Connor/Getty Images Entertainment/Getty Images; p. 19 Lisa Blumenfeld/Getty Images Sport/Getty Images; p. 21 Lester Cohen/Wire Image/Getty Images; p. 23 Tommaso Boddi/WireImage/Getty Images; p. 25 Jon Kopaloff/ FilmMagic/Getty Images; p. 27 Andrew H. Walker/Getty Images Entertainment/Getty Images; p. 29 Bennett Raglin/Getty Images Entertainment/Getty Images.

Printed in the United States of America

CPSIA compliance information: Batch #CS13GS: For further information contact Gareth Stevens, New York, New York at 1-800-542-2595.

Contents

Young Performer

Jordin Sparks is a singer and actor. She began singing and acting at a young age. She was just 17 when she won *American Idol*!

Beginnings

Jordin was born on December 22, 1989, in Phoenix, Arizona. Jordin's father was a football player. That meant the family moved around a lot.

Phillippi Sparks

Jordin started to sing when she was 18 months old! When she was 4, she entered singing contests. She wowed people.

Jordin started acting when she was 13.
She was in *The Wiz*, *Cinderella*, and
A Christmas Carol.

Early Album

Jordin recorded five songs on an album called *For Now*. A singer named Michael W. Smith asked her to sing in his shows.

Talent Shows

Jordin tried to get on TV talent shows such as *Star Search*. She loved singing in front of people.

In 2004, Jordin was on the show *America's Most Talented Kid*. She did well, but she didn't win.

American Idol

In 2006, Jordin tried out for *American Idol.* She sang "Because You Loved Me." The judges loved it!

Jordin spent months singing different songs on *American Idol.* In 2007, she was named the winner!

The Hits

Jordin soon put out an album called *Jordin Sparks*. Two famous songs on it are "Tattoo" and "No Air." Both were top-10 hits.

Jordin's next album was called *Battlefield*. It was another hit. She made songs people wanted to dance to.

25

On Stage and Screen

In 2010, Jordin made another dream come true. She was in a play on Broadway called *In the Heights*.

In 2012, Jordin was in the movie *Sparkle*. She sang and acted. Jordin is very busy living her dream!

Timeline

1989 Jordin is born December 22 in Phoenix, Arizona.

1993 Jordin starts singing in contests.

2002 Jordin begins acting.

2003 Jordin puts out an album called *For Now*.

2004 Jordin is on *America's Most Talented Kid*.

2007 Jordin wins *American Idol* and puts out the album *Jordin Sparks*.

2009 The album *Battlefield* comes out.

2010 Jordin sings on Broadway.

2012 Jordin appears in the movie *Sparkle*.

Books

Marcovitz, Hal. *Jordin Sparks*. Broomall, PA: Mason Crest Publishers, 2010.

Orr, Tamra. *Jordin Sparks*. Hockessin, DE: Mitchell Lane Publishers, 2009.

Websites

Jordin Sparks

www.jordinsparks.com/us/home

Check out the official site for Jordin Sparks.

Jordin Sparks

www.people.com/people/jordin_sparks/

Find the latest news about Jordin.

Glossary

Broadway: an area of New York City in which many theaters are found

contest: a test of skills among people, usually for a prize

record: to make a copy of music that can be played again and again

talent: a gift or skill

Index